About the Author

With over thirty years of success in helping people and organisations to transform and achieve their purpose, Alan Forsyth is delighted to share his passion for transformation and learning with a broad audience. As a consultant, small business owner and teacher he worked with executives and leaders to achieve greater profitability. He helped transform many community organisations and has now founded and developed the sustainability of The Men of Leith Men's Shed, a charity dedicated to eliminating isolation for men in Edinburgh. One look at the rich selection of creative and observational writing on his website, www.followingforsth.com will convince you of his engaging style.

His pursuits in Scotland included performing with the Rock Choir, playing his African drum, travelling and developing friendships. A happily married man, he has now returned to Australia, his home and is enjoying being with his three grown sons, friends and colleagues once again. In addition to writing he intends to pursue charitable endeavours, making a contribution to reducing concerns facing young people.

Five Gifts Flourishing

Alan Forsyth

Five Gifts Flourishing

Olympia Publishers
London

www.olympiapublishers.com
OLYMPIA PAPERBACK EDITION

Copyright © Alan Forsyth 2021

The right of Alan Forsyth to be identified as author of
this work has been asserted in accordance with sections 77 and 78
of the Copyright, Designs and Patents Act 1988.

All Rights Reserved

No reproduction, copy or transmission of this publication
may be made without written permission.
No paragraph of this publication may be reproduced,
copied or transmitted save with the written permission of the
publisher, or in accordance with the provisions
of the Copyright Act 1956 (as amended).

Any person who commits any unauthorised act in relation to
this publication may be liable to criminal
prosecution and civil claims for damage.

A CIP catalogue record for this title is
available from the British Library.

ISBN: 978-1-78830-765-9

First Published in 2021

Olympia Publishers
Tallis House
2 Tallis Street
London
EC4Y 0AB

Printed in Great Britain

Dedication

This book would not exist if it was not for my wife challenging me in New York City almost four years ago. As we looked at a slim lego like structure that escaped forever into the sky, she suggested it was time I wrote my first book. I dedicate this first book to Linda and acknowledge the comprehensive support and love she has offered in its creation.

Acknowledgements

There were two people who played a key role in helping me refine and finesse the book. Many thanks to Linda Hardie and Greta Silcock who made such a comprehensive evaluation of the first text and provided detailed feedback. Additionally, there were a collection of good people who provided feedback on the content and helped me to complete the project. Bryan Silcock, Simon Hauser, Adam Martinelli, Alan Stewart, Alex Carosi, Linda Gidlund and Sandra Stachowicz.

Introduction – Gifts

This is for you; I hope you like it.

At some stage of your life you may have been given a gift that made you stop. A gift that made your heart sing. At other times you are likely to have been given gifts that made you wonder why. Why did they get me that? The sickly coloured t-shirt, memorabilia from a tacky tourist shop or bunch of flowers already wilting. What were they thinking?

The chances are that regardless of the occasion or, indeed, even without an occasion, you have been given a gift that, according to your standards, fell way short as a gift. You may have been polite at the time, accepting the offer in the moment and later, secreting the gift in the drawer designated to host useless things.

When you did receive gifts that were simply brilliant, just perfect for you, you may have reflected on the time and effort that was invested in the choice. A choice based on who you are and what would stand out as the ideal gift for you. Such gifts we elevate, we talk about, we incorporate in our lives. Such gifts we celebrate.

I received such a gift for my fiftieth birthday. We were not what you call wealthy at the time, yet my wife had organised a long weekend trip from Melbourne, on mainland Australia, to somewhere else in Australia. As I sat in the business class lounge sipping champagne, wondering what the destination would be, already this was special. Already this was a gift I would choose.

As we arrived on the lovely green island of Tasmania off the south coast of Australia, the gift was shaping up to be perfect. Then as we drove into the Freycinet National Park and could make out a huge stingray like structure nestled in the trees and hugging the bay, I knew that this gift would be exquisite. This was our accommodation for the next few days, the luxury, the sleek luminescence of the Sapphire resort.

You would think that this was enough, yet that's not all. Once settled in and celebratory drinks poured, my wife gave me an additional present, A4 in size and in a simple gift wrap.

This gift was a story with pictures. It was a story of my life lovingly and diligently compiled by my wife. I read it through a film of tears. It was truly the best gift I had ever received. As I have told others later on many occasions, the exquisiteness of the lovely hotel and the lure of the beautiful environment were easily surpassed by this gift of love.

The story illustrates how gifts can move us, transform us. But what if the gift that transforms is not just the beautiful portfolio of photos or the exquisite get away? What if it is you that delights? What if you are the gift?

Please consider this question carefully, and as you do so, please consider yourself as a gift. The premise is simple and powerful. You have gifts, many gifts. We all possess these special gifts, often without even knowing it. If we can discover, refine and incorporate our individual gifts more readily in our lives, we can also more often experience the joy that they bring to ourselves and to others.

As you discover your gifts using this book, you will also uncover vehicles for designing your life in a way that is meaningful and delivers genuine happiness. Your gifts of life hold deep meaning for yourself and others, and provide a compass for you to grow and flourish. Imagine how fruitful that could be for those around you.

I am grateful for years of study, achieving and standing on the shoulders of academic qualifications, reading, academic research and practical experience in organisational transformation, ontological coaching, counselling, teaching, leadership development and change management. Achieving success with all of the above has generated personal challenges for me and transformational learning. I am inviting you to benefit from my comprehensive learning and experience of over thirty years, exploring your gifts through my compelling stories and exercises.

I am also inviting you to benefit from my pain; as you will ascertain, life has left me deeply vulnerable at times. An ability to respond to crisis and remain intact and viable is as much a part of this text as simply crafting a life of genuine happiness.

The gifts that you bring to life will be equally as potent as the exquisite gifts I received for my fiftieth birthday. More so, your gifts last a lifetime, they develop and improve with time and intent.

The style and structure of this text is deliberately different from many other books in order to engage and maximise your learning. It is created in a way that is simple and action oriented, inviting you to contribute to it as you contribute to transforming your life. It is as much a textbook as it is a work book or journal that you can choose to share with just yourself and others. Perhaps a gift in itself.

Enjoy creating your own book for your life as you discover the gifts that you offer.

You will learn:
1. How you can define and declare the core gifts in your life.
2. How you can have your gifts help you to live the way you choose to live.

My interpretation, based on over thirty years of work in personal and organisational transformation, is that we all possess personal gifts. These gifts may be informed by our identity, our values, our personalities, our professions, our children, our spirituality or simply by who we choose to be in the moment. Regardless, we all have gifts whether we choose to acknowledge this or not. Possibly, we have just not discovered what our individual gifts are yet and how they might shape our lives.

Achieving clarity as to your core gifts provides clarity and direction in your life. I am sure you either know of or have been yourself lost at some stage, unclear as to what to do and where to go in life. Such times can be stressful and have us experience what Buddhist psychology proposes as 'human suffering'. Being clear as to our direction in life is a potent antidote to human suffering.

> I watched with awe as my friend, John Williams, sitting at a snare drum in the Peanut Gallery Café, carefully observes a young woman about to perform a few numbers from her show at the Edinburgh Festival. She tentatively starts strumming her guitar and singing. John has never met this person, nor does he know what she will play, yet he intuits her performance and joins in seamlessly on the snare. His accompaniment is

exquisite and from the obvious smile of the young lady, is a welcome addition to her performance.

John is clear that one of his gifts is music, more specifically enjoying playing and performing with others. And like a carefully crafted song, he weaves this talent into his life, ensuring that he creates many opportunities to share and nurture his gift here in Edinburgh. Taking the occasional, respectful risk from time to time.

Developing a grounded understanding of your own core gifts can ease suffering significantly and open the way for you to develop a flourishing life.

As John will attest, singing and collaborating with others and playing joyfully provides significant relief from stress and a pathway to happiness for him.

I know it is not simple to take on personal development, change or transformation in your life.

Having supported many people: from youth to senior folks, community and educational groups, and corporate groups, through a journey of transformation, I agree it may not be easy. Yet it is indeed possible. Furthermore, it is worth it to engage in such transformation. You owe it to yourselves to improve your ways of being and fulfil your purpose.

By developing a solid understanding of your own gifts and developing a way of focussing your attention on these on a day to day basis, you will be better equipped for dealing with the everyday challenges of life. You will be able to better manage these and be ready to live a life that is more fulfilling, more flourishing.

This book provides solid practical ways in helping you

to move from clarity to action and ultimately to fulfilment. I will provide you with a number of tools and ideas to guide you along the way and some online support if you require it.

I will give you backstage passes to my life in terms of my gifts or, more accurately, my guides in life. Every day I create a map including each of my five gifts. They exist at the core of my day. Each gift is populated with tasks, commitments and outcomes culminating in me being guided purposefully through each and every day. In my Five Gifts Flourishing model, a diagram of which was introduced earlier, the central core of these images will be revealed and explained. I will also reveal through my own and others' stories, how I have uncovered or, indeed, discovered each gift and how I utilise the combination of gifts to craft my own fulfilling life.

Additionally, you will be given references, academic and otherwise, to research and intelligence that sit behind and inform this book. I readily acknowledge the great work of others who have influenced my thinking in creating this unique book.

My offer is to make transparent to you the reader, a selection of insights, theories and learnings from each of the professional domains I have participated in, making it easier for you to develop your own gifts and have them flourish. My five gifts are evident. Whatever the number of gifts you determine will be just right for you.

Beyond the theories and models, another way of starting to consider gifts is through stories. Here is a special story from my life around twenty years ago, when I started considering the role of gifts in my own life. I hope it resonates with you.

As I waded through the surging surf on Manly Beach,

pulled inexplicably by nature itself, I was reflecting on the truly amazing experience I had observed yesterday.

My colleagues from across the country and I had arrived at the last day of an intensive Neuro Linguistic Programming (NLP) training course. Popularised by John Grinder and Richard Bandler in the '70s, NLP training became a popular basis for personal and professional development with accreditation courses run across the world. Together with my colleagues, I found the content and delivery quite fascinating, challenging some of my thirty something ideas of life. Arriving in the training room we were all surprised that the space was empty with the exception of two short stacks of large sandstone bricks standing side by side. Sitting across the bricks was a piece of wood. Sitting beside this structure were a number of other carefully stacked pieces of wood.

In order to demonstrate the technique of meditation and focus, earlier in the course our instructors had shown how it was possible to actually break wood with our bare hands.

Now there was a palpable apprehension in the room as it was made apparent that we were actually going to do this. Yes, break wood with our bare hands. One by one my colleagues took on the challenge, coached by the instructors. One by one my colleagues did actually break the wood, each time the excitement and energy elevating in the room.

I stepped forward when the energy was at a peak, thinking I had mastered the breathing, the focus, the preparation to break through and... Slap, my hand bounced off the wood, smarting at the contact. My second attempt achieved the same outcome. I was letting myself and everyone down.

My heart racing, I was invited to focus all of my energies beyond the wood, to slow down my breathing, build my energy and embody strength.

Tears flowed the second I broke through, excitement levels increased to fever pitch and for the first time in my life I entered through the door of true possibility. I had just achieved something that I did not think I could do. My inability was confirmed by those two painfully failed attempts. But I did it. I did it!

Had I not have been willing to participate and willing to learn, I would not have walked through that doorway of opportunity in the first place. As I reflected, I realised that other doorways of opportunity had been there in my recent past, yet I had ignored them, or perhaps not even observed them. This was different, this time I walked through the door to a fresh future.

Whatever the doorway for you, I invite you to open it, to walk on through and start designing your own life. Your own gifts flourishing.

Like me in Sydney and, on many other occasions, where I have achieved what I formerly thought was impossible, I accepted help, I accepted coaching. You too will receive coaching through the process of transforming your life, throughout this text.

That said, it is essential that you turn up to your coaching sessions. By this I mean, a number of activities exist across the book. These have been carefully constructed and have solid evidence in research to take you from words to actions and, ultimately, success.

Please complete all exercises and please return to them for reflection.

If you are diligent in doing so, you maximise your chances of transforming your own life just the way you want to. I don't need to invite you to do this, I know. I know, you know, please just make it happen.

We will get started by exploring, firstly, the nature of gifts then progress the idea of flourishing.

This is for you! I do hope you like it.

Activities

You will note that there are a number of activities in the pages ahead, starting with the one below. Please complete the exercises, they have been carefully selected to enhance your reading experience and, more importantly, in achieving real and positive change in your life.

Similarly, there are several lined pages throughout. You could include ideas, thoughts, drawings, triggers and/or memories that come into your mind as you read. Please jot down whatever makes sense and is important to you, again it is your book and your choice.

Activity One
Now that you have read the introduction, I invite you to start work by answering a simple question. This page has been set aside specifically for your response, so please record your answer.

What's in it for you?

What benefits are available for you if you are to get clarity regarding your own gifts, your own life?

How might life be better for you?

For me, the benefit in taking control of my life was just that. For the first time in my life I was beginning to understand the importance of autonomy for me.

My experience with the breaking of the wood further acknowledged that breakthroughs were important in my life and in order for more to occur, I would need to be more focused on what I choose to achieve. And the process of achieving those breakthroughs may come with some discomfort or pain. However, it has certainly been worth it.

Why Gifts?

If we want to be able to create special, memorable gifts for ourselves, it is important that we first analyse the notion of gifts and gifting. Just like when we were learning how to cook for the first time, it was important to consider the steps, select the ingredients then follow the recipe.

A simple search of inspirational people will reveal a host of folks that not only all possess special gifts, but whose gifts are recognisable, unmistakable and sought after. Moreover, these people have found ways to have their gifts shine in their own worlds and in the wider world.

When you think of Winston Churchill, for example, what gifts come to mind?

How about Nelson Mandela or, indeed, the Dali Lama?

What about artists like Van Gogh, writers like Jane Austen, or performers like Elton John or Aretha Franklin?

Think for a moment about your own respected inspirational people and consider what gifts they have provided to themselves and humanity.

I invite you to also think about everyday people. Who has made a difference to you? Who are the everyday gift givers / contributors to you, your school, your community, your tribe?

> On the Short Hole Golf Course on Bruntsfield Links, Edinburgh, I was watching Jimmy recently, wearing an old stained pair of working overalls and manoeuvring a wheelbarrow full of rakes, spades, seed and varied hole cutting equipment. Jimmy is now in his senior years and every year at this time he helps the part time greenkeeper prepare the Short Hole Golf Course to come out of its winter hibernation. The course is free

and open to all during summer and Jimmy volunteers his time to ensure it is kept to a beautiful standard. Golf, as you will be aware, is important to Scotland and Jimmy is essential to the Short Hole Course in this part of Scotland, Bruntsfield Links.

He works away diligently, preparing the greens, marking the course, reseeding where necessary and re-digging the holes. This is the fifth year I have seen him do this and I am told that he has been doing it since he retired early in 1996.

I am impressed by his sense of service to the community and to the many tourists that play on this public course. I am also moved by his diligence. He is there several days every week in summertime, working from hole to hole regardless of the weather to make the course playable.

His contribution is for me one to be celebrated and acknowledged. There are some that drop their rubbish on the course, bend back the flag pins or simply disrespect the facility. This does not phase Jimmy, he is stoic, he is selfless, he delivers voluntarily for our community.

Every day leaders can assist us in refining and defining the gifts we choose to be remembered for and Jimmy is a sharp reminder of that.

Looking at gifts from an academic perspective, John Searle, an American philosopher and linguist, defined a number of speech acts that pepper our language without us necessarily knowing. One of his key speech acts, the act of offering, is of particular interest to us here. Put simply, when we deliver a gift, we make an offer.

As an offer, again according to Searle and other linguists, our gift can either be:
Accepted,
Declined, or
Renegotiated.
It is as simple as that.

As you know from the many gifts that have made it into the not so useful drawer, we do not immediately accept all gifts. Many we simply decline or reject. Given human nature, we also do not necessarily let people know that we have declined their gift, often politely saying thank you and looking the other way.

We have already identified well known and not so well-known people whose gifts we have accepted. How can we achieve the same level of acceptance for our gifts? How can we override a veneer of polite non-acceptance and achieve genuine acceptance for our gifts, a genuine acceptance of what we have to offer ourselves and the broader community?

The linguists reach out one more time. They interpret that once we have made an offer and that offer is accepted, we have a promise.

If we consider that the gifts that we are about to craft, ultimately become promises. Then, like our friend Jimmy, we are entering into an important contract with ourselves and others in pursuit of our flourishing life.

With this importance in mind, we will consider deeply our core life concerns, articulate our deep values and ultimately create gifts that are not only accepted by others but also provide daily guidance, helping us achieve meaning and genuine happiness in our life.

We will be making and keeping promises and discovering how deeply satisfying that can be.

Activity Two

What promises have you made in your life that you have kept? What has been the impact of keeping such promises?

Please also use the space below to write down any ideas you have generated as you reflect on the text so far.

A voice from the back seat.

We had left at four a.m., our three boys immediately going back to sleep in the back seat of the people mover, silence. This was another of our family holidays, a long drive from Melbourne, Australia, up the east coast to Queensland via Sydney. A few hours later, I filled the silence by listening to one of Steven Covey's audio tapes, discussing his seven habits theory.

Feeling a bit weary myself, I thought I might swap Covey for AC/DC and wake me up for another couple of hours driving. Immediately on pressing the stop button on the tape player, a small but insistent voice travelled from the back of the car. "I was listening to that," declared Duncan, then only eight years old.

Such was the impact of Steven Covey that he even captured the attention of my children when I was becoming a little less focussed.

I had the opportunity to meet him in the mid-nineties following his presentation at Dallas Brooks Hall in Melbourne. There were three ideas he put forward that at the time assisted greatly in my journey in personal development.

The first was his compelling invitation to 'Be islands of excellence in a sea of mediocrity'. He then introduced the notion of a compass, a life compass encouraging us to find our own true north. The third idea that stuck with me was his statement: 'Don't get caught in the thick of thin things'.

These three ideas became a foundation for me in living a life more out of importance than urgency. Developing the ingredients of focus, excellence and accomplishment. I share these ideas here to acknowledge an important influence in my life transformation and, as an agent, assisting others in transformation and change.

As we continue to explore your gifts and your gifts' flourishing, I invite you to think about Steven Covey's challenge around excellence. What are areas of your life that would benefit by you simply raising the standards? Being a model for your goals that not only you but others could also aspire to.

The following events occurred at a time in my life where I was realising that, rather than simply coasting through life, I could instead embrace it. I had that choice available to me. I include the story here to remind me of my ongoing quest. I also employ it to support you with your quest.

How can you be an island of excellence?

New Tools – New Gifts.

One of the tools I wanted to add to my own coaching tool box was the well-known personality type inventory, the MBTI, or the Myer Briggs Type Inventory. Influenced by my own observations in working with different people and guiding them through positive change, I agreed with Isabell Briggs Myers and Katherine Cook Briggs in their book Gifts Differing, when they said, 'Yet we cannot safely assume that other people's minds work on the same principles as our own'. P1.

In my early consulting days, I was keen to add to my post graduate qualification in organisation a change by achieving a qualification that would accredit me to use the MBTI psychological inventory with my clients. I agreed with the principles of diversity explored by the Myers team and was looking for a method of uncovering personal value / strengths in my clients. The process of gaining qualification again allowed me to walk through another door of possibility. It allowed me to challenge my previous mediocrity as a student and develop new standards of attainment. It also challenged me in that if I were to achieve higher standards in this instance, how could I consistently sustain such standards in other areas of my life?

I discovered that in order to achieve accreditation to use the MBTI, I would need to attend a four-day course and sit a two-hour exam. Imagine the fear I experienced when I discovered that I required a pass grade of 95% on the exam. At best in my life as a student, I had only ever achieved 55% under exam situations. I just scraped through to gain my Higher School Certificate a couple of decades ago with just over 50%. Aiming to almost double this grade seemed impossible. Could I achieve this?

Oddly enough, I did have some recently acquired resources available to me. I had been learning how to learn. I had joined the Accelerated Learning Society of Australia and attended Stephanie Burns dynamic Learning to Learn weekend. With additional reading, conversations and coaching, I discovered that I was able to learn the contents of the MBTI course in a way that was compatible with, and actually preferred by my brain. For the first time in my life I was learning to record, interpret and recall information in a way that met my needs. This was refreshing and empowering.

I had been practising recording information in ways compatible to my brain's preferences, adopting mind mapping as my preferred tool of capturing and memorising information. Previously, I had taken linear notes that I simply did not remember sufficiently well in test situations. I found with mind mapping techniques, I was able in exam contexts to record and recall information more readily and more accurately.

My discovery at how powerful this was arrived when I opened the envelope with the certificate of results for the MBTI course. I scored over 99 out of 100. Remarkable!

Put simply, here was another doorway opening up to me, a doorway to academic scores I never thought would be possible for me.

In addition to challenging my existing standards, I was also in the question of how I could sustain higher levels of performance and truly flourish in times ahead. The MBTI exam story demonstrates how it is possible to give attention to what we regard as important and even if we have not done so ever before, develop the skills and motivation to rise to the occasion when required. It also suggests that if we are to be 'islands of excellence', this cannot be a once off performance. We need to find ways to continually, consistently and sustainably have our dreams shine.

My fundamental suggestion here is that you identify your fresh skills or strategies, combine them with what already works and find ways to make them habitual. As you will see from my Five Gifts Flourishing model, I track each gift on a daily basis. This ensures that my activity is invested regularly across my gifts and each develops in sync. These are gifts for now, and in perpetuity.

We will talk more about attention later in this text, especially from a mindfulness perspective. For now, if we can simply consider how we can be more attentive, focussed on each of our gifts daily, it is far more likely that they will be nourished and indeed flourish.

So far, we have considered:

- We all have gifts.
- Gifts can be offers and ultimately promises that can be kept for ourselves and others.
- The importance of excellence and focus in our lives.
- Gifts, when nimbly crafted and nurtured on a daily basis can truly improve our current and future life.

We will be considering more elements as we progress from simply exploring our gifts to actually putting them into action in our lives. Like any significant journey, I want you to be absolutely prepared before you leave.

Language is Important in Putting Your Gifts to Work

The language I have been using in this text and my Five Gifts Flourishing model is considered, chosen carefully to elevate the importance of our quest here, and to provide clarity and direction to our journey forward. The whole notion of gifts and their flourishing existence is not a pedestrian activity. It requires carefully chosen language, sometimes eloquent and certainly engaging. I include this discussion on the important role of language to incorporate more recent thoughts in the areas of positive psychology, emotional intelligence, ontology and mindfulness. These domains are not exclusive but do contribute to the role language plays on what we observe and achieve in our lives.

Language is extremely important. 'The limits of my language means the limits of my world', Ludwig Wittgenstein. Wittgenstein, who taught language at the University of Cambridge, was considered an expert in the philosophy of mind and language. He echoed the linguists I discussed earlier who similarly would go on to say that whilst we are limited by the language we have available to us, we can use our existing language more cleverly.

Effectively, what I am inviting you to take on here, is developing a language that helps you define your gifts and helps you articulate them in ways that facilitate their achievement.

The utility of language can be illustrated by the following quote, often attributed to Anthony Robbins, yet equally mentioned by others.

'Energy flows where the attention goes!'.

During the early 2000s, the term BHAGs became popular in organisations. A B.H.A.G. is a Big, Hairy, Audacious Goal. The term may appear a tad ridiculous, yet the central nervous system is not all that concerned with how big, how hairy or how audacious your goals or intentions are. Our central nervous system can allow for energy and effort to flow in the direction of our attention or intention regardless of size.

Put simply, if your daily attention is on ways at which you can just get by in life, then there is a greater chance of you doing just that; just getting by. If instead you are focused, as Wittgenstein suggests, on expanding your world through your language, especially on a daily basis, then you are better equipped to lead a life more meaningful.

The reason I raise this orientation and use words like gifts and flourishing is simply to declare a possibility. We create possibilities in our lives, doorways to walk through as previously described. We can also be assisted or severely limited by how we present them in our language.

Whatever your aspirations, I invite you to consider using language that aptly defines and expresses the extent of your aspiration. I referred earlier to Stephen Covey in the context of how we can flourish. We can do so with our language, as

Mr Covey encourages, 'Be islands of excellence in a sea of mediocrity'.

Rather than water down your intentions with mediocre language, simply use language that enrols and excites. Your central nervous system is as open to being entertained as you are.

I found a great example when working within a substantial telecommunications organisation helping managers and leaders to transform their leadership skills and improve their performance. Regularly, I would ask senior staff the question, "How are you?" Inevitably, the response would be an emphatic, "Busy!", with an obligatory shrug of the shoulders. I recorded their answers.

At the time, there existed on the bookshelves of children's bookshops a series called 'Mr Men'. One of the Mr. Men books was called, 'Mr Busy'. I bought a number of copies of this text and handed it out to the leaders I was working with during our coaching sessions. I would invite the leaders to read the short text and answer the question, "What is Mr Busy good at?"

Inevitably, the leaders would answer in overwhelming agreement, "He is good at being busy." They understood the point immediately, that Mr Busy's orientation towards busy seeped into his language and ultimately his behaviour. On returning to their earlier response to the question, "How are you?", different language choices were now considered by the leaders.

Additionally, simply being good at being busy was not an effective leadership competence at the time. Interestingly, the idea of being busy had developed such a currency in their language and in the organisation's lexicon that it had almost developed a desirable status.

I encouraged them to take more care, pay more attention to

their choice of words and introduced them to the suggestopedic nature of language as defined by R. J. George Lozanov.

Lozanov developed a method of teaching languages he called suggestopedia. What we can learn from this is that embedded language commands can be utilised that make us more open to learning or suggestion. Commands that are, let's say, more appealing to the central nervous system.

We use this as parents daily: for example, 'do you want to go to bed with a short story, or stay up for ten minutes more, without the story?'. The outcome is the same... bed in ten minutes. We have effectively embedded simple suggestopedia type language commands in a short sentence.

Let us go back to the senior staff in the telecommunications company. Their range of answers to the same question, "How are you?" had now changed to the following.

Contemplative,

Focussed,

Purposeful,

On track,

A bit rushed today yet generally achieving outcomes,

Excited,

Productive.

Leaders understood how easy it was to be trapped in habitual language patterns and, more importantly, limited language patterns. Through coaching in attention, priority management and effective organisation of commitments, it was possible to shift management behaviours from being reactive and limited to being responsive, considered and proactive.

You have control over your language and as suggested here can expand your skills to better facilitate the creation of your gifts.

What are you now going to promise to yourself? From

what you have read so far, what makes sense to you as the first of your life gifts to identify and pursue? And how might you articulate that? Here is a language activity to assist.

Activity Three. How are you?
What do you say habitually? If you can't think of anything, ask people who know you well.

What could you say?

What are other things you say habitually, for example in answer to the question, what do you do?

What could you say differently that could enrol or engage people in your ideas?

Are you well enough to read and benefit from this book and am I well enough to write this book?

Whilst this is not a book written specifically from a mental illness or mental health perspective, it is written from a learning perspective and assumes that no matter what our challenges, mental, physical or otherwise, we all have the capacity to learn.

You could easily ask the question, was I well enough to compose this book? At times, given my own challenges with mental illness, there have been moments when it has been hard enough to simply get into the shower than actually sit down and write something meaningful.

Colleagues of mine in Australia who are associated with the impressive charity, Beyond Blue, have successfully campaigned to have the broader community accept that it is OK to not be OK. Yes, it is OK not to be OK.

Part of being a learner is to recognise not just who we are but how we are, what core moods we are inhabiting and how these allow or limit us from achieving our future intent.

The right conversation in the wrong mood may well be the wrong conversation.

Wherever we are on the spectrum, whether or not a spectrum exists, and on whatever day or given moment, you will know what is possible for you. Perhaps it is just one thing today, perhaps it is many. You choose the pace to immerse yourself in this reading, a pace that is OK for you.

In the previous chapter I explored the importance of language. Our behaviours can be considerably impacted by the language we use to define ourselves or others. It is easy to use labels as a convenient way to describe a set of behaviours that define our humanness. Or, in clinical / medical settings to describe a condition and therefore dictate appropriate means for recovery.

For now, and as you read this text, I would encourage you to label yourselves simply as learners or a similar label that allows you to engage with curiosity.

As a previous General Manager and now Chairman of Men's Sheds, I have regularly had professionals approach me to determine if it is appropriate that their clients join a Men's Sheds. They typically describe their clients according to their diagnosis and not, as I have discovered, the deep, unique characters they are. I have had many men, who were previously described as Manic Depressive, Schizophrenic, Chronically Depressive and so on, become members in our sheds and benefit from being able to dilute the labels.

What typically happens in the shed communities is that whilst the labels remain outside the doors of the sheds in the sheds, the men are embraced by other members of the sheds for who they are, simply men. Some men have many challenges, some perhaps fewer; they are all legitimate men.

The reason I include this learning is to highlight my observations that labels can be useful to inform strategies for improvement, they can also be disastrous when they restrict us in dealing with people as people, not as people who have a mental illness.

As I stated earlier, if you have a diagnosis and that in some ways informs you as to your challenges and how to deal with them, great. I am simply inviting you to put labels aside as you proceed through this text in the spirit of learning. Not to ignore it. Certainly not, yet also, not to embrace it as if it is the all-encompassing truth for you and who you are. You are a learner.

> My long term friend and former business partner, Mark Molony, was diagnosed with bowel cancer in his early thirties. A young father and devout family man, Mark was devastated by this diagnosis. It took him a while, as it does with all of us faced with similar predicaments, to accept such a diagnosis. Mark is an incredibly powerful learner who yes, at that point in time, had bowel cancer.
>
> I will never forget my visit with him shortly before his surgery. I understand that there is now an online application where you can load up a photo of yourself and it gives you a predicted version of what you will look like twenty to thirty years later. When I visited Mark in hospital just before his surgery, he actually looked twenty to thirty years older.
>
> He was preparing for his surgery and had pictures, mind maps and drawings from all of his family surrounding him. He had also determined a strategy he

was going to use leading up to the operation. Passionate about the role of the mind in healing and passionate about learning, Mark was planning to isolate himself, go into a meditative state, and one by one imagine that all of the people he knew and loved in his world would visit him and he would speak with them one by one.

I am not suggesting that isolation was a key here, Mark had a number of self-management strategies that he could control, that he could use in his life beyond the medical interventions. Utilising these together with conventional medicine he survived cancer.

His remarkable survival led him to an equally remarkable achievement just two years ago as he proceeded to donate his kidney to his brother.

Amongst other pursuits, Mark now coaches people with a cancer diagnosis. Part of his coaching has them accept their diagnosis, not fight against it. Instead, he invites them to discover, as he did, other ways in their minds, in their language and in their bodies that they can effect a positive change in their wellbeing and improve their bodies' capacity to heal.

Mark is currently writing a book on recovery coaching.

In the meantime, we can learn to accept labels and we can also explore new ways of responding to and responding beyond our challenges, beyond the labels themselves. Again, as learners, I invite you to do both.

So, I believe we are all eligible to read and benefit from this book, just as I am absolutely equipped to write it.

My Five Gifts

Hitherto, we have set out a compelling set of reasons for you to identify and create your gifts.

You have been entertained by a few stories and exercises of how you can make a start on defining your own gifts, conscious of the role of language and the power of an offer that could be accepted.

You have also been encouraged by great writers like Stephen Covey and Wittgenstein not to water your offer down, rather than for your gifts to be the best they can be.

Now, I will begin to unwrap the detail of each of my five gifts, taking you on a tour of how each of them evolved and introducing a key theory or model underpinning them. For each of the five you will be introduced to a key activity aimed at helping you define, articulate and establish your own gifts.

The activities have been central to my definition and expression of my five gifts, and will provide a starting point for you.

Beyond this, I will be introducing you to other powerful exercises to help with your definition and expression of yourself, your gifts. These activities have been selected carefully and presented in an order to assist you with your focus and attention.

My five gifts are depicted as a series of images, images I carry with me every day to remind me of their presence and luminance. The five gifts are:
1. Relationships and family. Underpinned by conversation, collaboration and community.
2. Well-being including mindfulness.
3. Charity balanced with wealth.
4. Learning.
5. Creativity.

In a previous section on flourishing, I closed by suggesting our intention and focus had palpable influence on what we could achieve. I bring this up again to provide a context for my own gifts and how I was able to define and ultimately live out of them.

As an adolescent and a younger man, I had no real sense of potential in my life. Already, I have shared two stories of events that opened the door to potential and possibility for me. At these stages I developed an openness for, and an understanding of, the power of goals and goal orientation.

Before I discovered this, I was caught by just getting by. Perhaps it was the high school I went to where violence seemed to be so much a part of the school you could be mistaken to think it was on the curriculum. At best I attempted to avoid being a target.

'Welcome to Lyndale High School' said the banner on the gym hall; Lyndale was a reasonably new school near Dandenong in Australia, built to cater for an increasing population of immigrants. The big red letters suggested that this new school may be all right.

I had arrived recently with my family having spent two glorious years in Georgetown, Tasmania. There was the bush, the bikes and ample opportunities to play in this small friendly town. Everything you could hope for as a ten year old.

Now, at age twelve, I was tentatively walking down the main corridor of the school. My uniform was so new it was uncomfortable. You will get used to it, Mum had said. I continued down the corridor passing banks of grey lockers and triangular flags. As I approached the staff room and the Principal's office, kids and school bags seemed to pour in from the playground.

I experienced a sudden pain, falling to the ground and gasping for air. I had been kicked viciously in the stomach simply for being there. Yes, welcome to Lyndale High School.

Whilst I was never attacked so viciously again, my early years at high school were dampened by fear. This was not a place for potential. This was not a place to showcase my creativity and expression.

Given these limited opportunities, I simply got on with life, playing down any creative pursuits I quietly might have hoped for. Those dreams were the confines of TV shows like Countdown or Johnny Youngs Young Talent Time. Perhaps it was a current social narrative that impressed on me that when you left school or university you got a job, any job. Despite a lack of any preparation for finding a job, I did get a few jobs; I pressed on according to this limited expectation, filling paint tins in a factory and failing as a sales consultant in a role that I clearly was not suited for or passionate about.

Whatever our background, if we are not aware of or encouraged in our potential, we may become completely unaware of our potential, or the potential we can foster and create for ourselves. Instead, like me, I simply smiled weakly or grimaced and just on with it.

Regardless of this limiting background, I was still able to shift from a restricted notion of myself to a more bullish notion. Throughout my life, particularly beyond school and university, this notion that I could actually make a difference started to emerge, to grow and to prosper. Now, it flourishes.

As we explore each of my gifts, I will articulate the corresponding events or the breakthroughs that occurred to establish my now fulfilling life.

As I carefully unwrap each of my five gifts with you, I will provide a context as to how I shifted from just getting on with things to actually making things happen. I will explore the conditions with you that have worked and are working for me. And, more importantly, I will outline steps for you to follow in designing your gifts.

Gift One: Nurturing Family & Relationships through Community, Conversation and Collaboration.

In this, my first gift, I will introduce you to two substantial exercises that I believe will be of enormous benefit to you. The first is an analysis of your values, the second a solid exploration of the core concerns you experience.

We will explore the three C's that underpin Family & Relationships and are at the core of achieving any gift. The three Cs are: community, conversation and collaboration. These will be explored in detail later in the book.

I share this next story with you to highlight an important discovery for me. This was the first time I had a sense of how potent, how transformational, finding some of my core values was on my life.

I could tell that the NYLEX clock was just starting to lose its luminescence as the morning light filtered through. It was still prominent though, sitting atop the wheat silo with its billion-dollar view over the Yarra River, Botanic Gardens and Melbourne itself. This was a new day, not just any day; this was my first son, Callum's, actual birthday.

I was holding him, a little tentatively, for the first time and reflecting over the rollercoaster of events that commenced with my wife almost breaking her waters at a local Thai restaurant. Now, almost forty-eight hours later there was the brutality and beauty of birth. The seemingly never-ending contractions and my cutting of the umbilical cord through a small waterfall of tears.

And that is the point, I had never really cried like this ever before. I had never been touched so deeply as this. My whole notion of life started to disintegrate then reassemble in a fresh way.

It was at that point as I sat in joyful, silent tears with my new son that I comprehended a truly different way of being. Life, it was now different. Within a month of that moment, I was more than just talking about the value of family and relationship in my life, I was living a big change.

I was telling people that I was going to be a stay at home dad. Actually, living out these new values I had discovered in family and relationship. To deepen my involvement in these areas, by being present and choosing to be a primary care giver. A decision that, back then, was still uncharted and not often welcome territory for men.

I still reflect on this decision as one of the best I have made in my life, it allowed me to achieve a genuine experience that was authentic to me. It also set me on a lifelong journey to live a life constructed in a way that my actions directly correlated to my values. I was living in service of them.

For decades, I have been undertaking an exploration into individuals' values, what they determine is of core to them and truly important. This sifting process has been illuminating with many of the people I have introduced it to. Often, they will say that it provided them with insight, clarity and motivation to focus on what is most important to them, to change and to thrive.

For me, like the wood breaking and the near perfect score on the MBTI test, this was another doorway opening experience. I knew that to embrace the gifts of family and relationships fully in my life, it would create a fundamentally more powerful identity and possibilities for me.

Often, we discover our core values when we notice something is not quite right. Have you ever had that feeling when something is awry? Perhaps you have been asked to do something that does not feel right or go somewhere that does not make sense. Perhaps what you are observing is contrary to, or clashing, with your own values in some way.

Equally, when our values are aligned with our behaviours and actions, we can feel that we are in a good place, an authentic place.

Activity Four. Values Elicitation – Idea to Action
There are a number of self-help books that give you a list of values and ask you to select those that you think are important. I am going to suggest an alternative and, I believe, more potent approach. It will involve some work on your part.

Start with the question:
What is important to you about life?

Be persistent; keep asking the question until you get an answer that makes sense, e.g. family, prosperity, travel, health, etc.

Make sure you record your answers on the page provided. Consider your responses; add or delete or amend as you feel appropriate.

With each remaining answer on the list, apply the following question:

What is really important to you about each answer on the list?

Keep asking this new question until you are getting frustrated by the question. Pester yourself with the questions until you have around six to nine responses.

Take each of the responses one more time,
asking the question:
What is really important to me about this?

Once you are satisfied with your six to nine responses, list them in order of importance to you.

A useful question here is:
Is freedom more important than vitality?
OK, if so, is vitality more important that child welfare?
Keep going until you have them in order from 1 to 9.

You are likely by now to have nine core values derived through some good work on your behalf.

For each of the values you have identified,
apply the following test:
In order to feel value 2, this would have to happen.
Apply this test for each value listed.
Review your work. Read them back to yourself in order. Do they make sense?

From Values to Concerns

Stephen Covey, mentioned earlier, suggests that when we are exploring our personal development, we should 'begin with the end in mind'.

Using another highly practical tool, we are going to consider our own end in mind. What could that be?

Fernando Flores and Michael Graves in their seminal work on Domains of Human Concern, identified thirteen areas of life of core concern that show up for people as differing priorities. The idea is that, whether we are aware of these or not, they sit in the background and influence our choices throughout life.

I include them here for you to begin to contemplate your end state. What does it say on this list of thirteen, that is of ultimate importance to you and why?

Please use the activity worksheet to work through and identify your priorities in life.

Activity Five. Human Concerns and You
Of the listed concerns identified by Graves & Flores what are the few, say two or three, that resonate most with you? Of those two or three, what do you notice are present for you or missing from your life?

1. *Body – health, sickness, vitality, availability for meetings, functions, events.*
2. *Play or aesthetics entertainment, recreation, art, art appreciation.*
3. *Sociability – making, maintaining and breaking friendships, trust building.*
4. *Family – marriage, having children, educating children, caring for family members.*
5. *Work – doing your job, completing actions you have committed to.*
6. *Education – gaining competence and skill in some area.*
7. *Career – choosing a direction in life, a career or profession to prepare for and follow.*

8. *Money – having enough to support you, salary, reputation with others.*
9. *Membership – participation in clubs, organisations, citizenship.*
10. *World – politics, environment, other countries and culture.*
11. *Dignity – Self-respect, self-esteem, living up to your own standards.*
12. *Situation – disposition, temperament, outlook, emotions, how things are going.*
13. *Spirituality, philosophy, religion, finding meaning in life.*

I will relate a personal experience that brings this enquiry to life. Long before I had encountered the work of Flores, Graves and also a man by the name of Humberto Maturana, my wife and I were in conversation around how we might approach the education of our currently unborn children. We were both passionate about providing any future children with opportunities in learning that we perceived were missing in our own educations.

What I found interesting was the number of decisions we would make, often without even knowing, what would in the future facilitate a better education. Or better career prospects for our children compared to what we had experienced ourselves.

Similarly, when I discovered the previous model, I was surprised at the myriad of decisions we had made across our lives. Decisions that were to allow time and space with family and opportunities for sociability. Family and sociability are both domains that are central to my life now and feature in my first gift. I embrace their importance in my life.

A recent interview with a friend encouraged me to reflect on these values again. The transcript below demonstrates their ongoing importance. An earlier version of me would find it quite challenging to simply accept this feedback without recoiling in embarrassment. I include the transcript here as an example of how others perceive my values in action.

"Lastly, and perhaps most importantly I see you at your best when you are with your family. You are completely dedicated to loving and supporting Linda and your sons (and your extended family). The value that you add to their lives as a husband, a father and a brother simply cannot be measured. I see the way you lovingly prepare the evening meals – whether it's for two or twenty and or take care of the projects at home (here or abroad) that just have to get done. Your level of dedication is complete. Developing and maintaining a sense of family (or community) is paramount. You always light up when you've got plans for people coming over – and then I surely see you at your best. I can tell how much you value and protect time for those you love. You are always at your best when you are hosting relatives or friends, despite whether or not it's been for one day too many or one day too few. You treat everyone in your life with the love and respect that they deserve as a human being (and as part of a broader human family). No questions asked." Adam Martinelli

Activity Six. Combining Values & Core Concerns.
Looking at your life from the perspectives of values and concerns, what key themes do you notice that emerged from the last two activities?
Remember your gifts are your core offer.
What values should be included at the centre of your

gifts? What values will you choose to focus on that define you?

What concerns will you include in your gifts?

How can your concerns help inform what your offer and what your gifts should be?

Eight worldly concerns

In my recent studies into mindfulness with the excellent Mindful Life Program (MLP) facilitated in the U.S. I was introduced to a very useful model, derived from Buddhist practices, that helps us to find our track and stay on track.

The eight concerns model helps us to create accurate, reality-based perceptions of ourselves.

Taken from the companion guide to the Mindful Life Program the eight worldly concerns are:

Gain and Loss – In order to get what we want and avoid loss we can invest an inordinate amount of time.

Pleasure and Pain – Seeking pleasure and avoiding pain is natural yet not healthy if only undertaken for short term reasons.

Praise and Criticism – To be validated or legitimised is important, yet it can become obsessive.

Good and Bad Reputation – An overt concern with the number of friends someone has on Facebook or similar short-term assessments on similar social media platforms illustrates just how obsessed and fickle our sense of reputation may be.

I include the eight worldly concerns to highlight how easy it is for us to be obsessed by stimulus driven, short term pleasures or sufferings. When considering your gifts, I invite you to think beyond these. Consider what is really important here.

Another question I often asked clients to consider is, "For the sake of what?" For the sake of what is that important to you?

Clarity around how you choose to live your life will assist enormously in contributing to genuine long-term happiness, not a brief sense of pleasure achieved through temporary considerations.

Activity Seven. Eight Worldly Concerns
When faced with all, or some, of these driving forces what healthy decisions can you make?

Are there any particular worldly concerns that are more a driving force than you would choose?

What can you do to be aware of and change this?

For the sake of what is that particular concern important to you?

_____

_____

_____

_____

_____

_____

_____

_____

_____

Gift Two : Well-being!

I aim to live healthily adopting a spirit of Well-being.

Most of us would agree that our health is a gift, not a given. I am informed by the Buddhist / mindfulness notion of three thoughts. Firstly, it is important to regularly consider what we are grateful for and secondly, it is useful for us to contemplate the notion of impermanence. We will die, we just don't know when or under what circumstances. Not that this is a morbid pursuit, more a platform for us to consider the third thought, the here and now and how we best use our time, in pursuit of our gifts in the present.

My focus on health and well-being commenced in my early twenties and has continued into my early sixties. I have had a few major health breakdowns in between these times so feel equipped to share some distinctions that may assist you in crafting a similar gift focussed on the mind and body.

There are two foundational practices I would like to introduce here that, like values and concerns, will assist you enormously in defining, articulating and living your gifts.

The two practices are:

Attention, where this involves our focus and intent, e.g. living an intentional life as opposed to just going with the flow, and,

Meditation, a practice of training the mind to be present.

Both are integral to my current well-being and capacity to thrive in each of my five gifts.

I started to discover the power of attention and intention in my thirties following studies into learning and organisational change. Again, these realisations provided me more opportunities to walk through doors of possibility. Here is a story from that time, reinforcing the importance of attention in relation to achievement.

"I am sorry, mate, I can't do it, I have an injury and have been told not to compete." Immediately I was gutted. There were only two weeks to go until I was to compete in my first half marathon on the Gold Coast in Queensland, Australia and my running mate had just pulled out.

Here were the facts: I had never done anything like this before, I too was recovering from an infection. However, I had told so many people that I would do it and put in a hell of a lot of training including running up and down the stunning Mount Gravatt with our family dog, Melba.

At the time of competing in this and other long-distance running events, I was supported by making compelling goals. My study in accelerated learning and Neuro Linguistic Programming had encouraged me to focus on the power of language, external and internal dialogue. It had also allowed me to focus on using more specific language aligned to goal achievement.

SMART goals was one of the models I was using at that time and whilst that may grate with many of you, I found that it was also possible to create a rigorous goal and have not just your conscious mind but your unconscious mind also kicking in for you with support. I was reading and practising methods of engaging a whole brained approach to setting and achieving goals.

Specific – Your goal should be as clear as possible – see 1 below.

Measurable – You should easily be able to determine whether you have succeeded or not – 1 and 2 below.

Accepted / agreed – Where others are required to make it happen or help make it happen, this should be noted and collaboration secured. In this case I had the support of my wife, aligning our schedules so I had the time necessary to train and compete.

Realistic – There is not much point taking on a goal that is impossible. In my case, others had done it under similar circumstances. So, it was possible.

Time framed – See 1 & 2 below.

So, my goal for the half marathon was very clear.
1. Complete the course without stopping in under two hours.
2. Be able to run again within forty-eight hours of competing.

I used all of the tools I had at my disposal including breaking down the goal into sensible stages with a tiered exercise plan.

At the end of each practice run I created an anchor, a method I had discovered in my Neuro Linguistic Programming mastery training. This was based on associating a specific physical action, say a clap of the hands, with a moment of feeling good having just finished vigorous exercise. The premise was that the more you created the association, the more the central nervous system would hotwire it. Allowing you to use the trigger even when you were not exercising. Effectively tricking the brain into feeling more prepared.

I fed my unconscious mind with stories of people who had achieved similar things, often considering these achievements just short of sleep. The idea was that the unconscious mind would embed the stories during sleep, in my dreams if you like. The benefit of these stories would then be available during waking times.

The result was I completed the course in one hour and forty-eight minutes; headed off to the airport that evening for a flight to Melbourne; and was, albeit tentatively, running again the following morning. SMART goal achieved.

This whole brained approach to setting and achieving goals is palpable. It has served me well in achieving health and recovery goals I never knew were possible. More doorways to step through.

Attention Mindfulness & Meditation

One of the definitions of mindfulness I found in my recent studies was being aware of our mental states without being caught by them.

B. Alan Wallace, www.alanwallace.org, author and expert on Tibetan Buddhism, refers in his Ted Talk to us as having 'Monkey Minds', minds that do not cease chattering. Minds that are not aware of our mental state and as the metaphor suggests, absolutely caught. He goes further to suggest that we are impaired by minds that are obsessive, compulsive and delusional, consistently distracting us, consistently demanding our attention.

His invitation is that if we can genuinely calm or tame our minds, we can make healthier choices.

So, in this context we will explore ways in which we can sharpen our attentiveness using mindfulness and meditation as vehicles to improve our health and reduce the chattering.

Daniel Goldman and Richard Davidson in their video, 'Does Mindfulness Really Work', found on YouTube 9th September, 2017, discuss the effectiveness of mindfulness.

Identifying six thousand peer reviewed articles and focussing on sixty of these, they summarise the results and arrive at an alternative definition.

Mindfulness is a method of training your attention to keep it where you want to, avoiding distractions and diversions.

Effectively I, like Goleman and Davidson, am encouraging you to sharpen your attention, to avoid distractions and diversions, to calm your mind and prepare it to be attentive.

What they find is:
- We are a highly distracted culture.
- Eight weeks of training can produce a change in focus. Having the mind wander less, and become more focussed.
- We can train the mind to 'tone down' the executive centre of the brain.
- We can increase retention.
- We can strengthen the prefrontal cortex (executive centre) to say no.

- Mindfulness helps with self-management and self-confidence.

Goleman and Davidson recommend practising meditation and mindfulness every day for at least thirty days to help build a resilient habit. I did just that, accepting the offer of the Mindful Life Program, to be guided in meditation every day for a month. Meditation is now a daily practice for me.

Mindfulness and Me – The Back Story

I am keen to outline the benefits of living with mindfulness, yet before I do so, here is an outline of some of the challenges I faced before being introduced to such practices.

Life has not always been so buoyant for me.

I am sure you have had one of those dreams where you have struggled to get out of a place only to be released when you wake up, relieved. My struggle to escape used to occur in real life. Often enough for me to be able to be reminded by how powerless I felt. It was like I was pushed up against the stage at a huge rock concert, drowning in the volume of people and music, with no ability to get out.

This was one of a multitude of feelings I experienced shortly after being diagnosed with a mental illness, bipolar disorder. For a number of years, I would swing from mania to depression. From a vanilla existence to something in between. Despite being prescribed a drug therapy, I experienced little escape from these extremes. In short, life was pretty ordinary for me for quite a number of years.

I would fly on business trips to Sydney on a whim and with no appointments made, and no real reason to be there.

I commissioned a work of art entitled 'Identity' with no way to pay for it.

I would drive fast and erratically, luckily causing no damage to others or myself.

I would park my work vehicle late in the afternoon and sleep in the driver's seat in a haze of disappointment.

I rarely wanted to get out of bed in the morning.

I would sit in the psychiatrist's waiting room. Dreading being there, but not knowing where to go or what to do instead.

In fifteen years, I have discovered many strategies to help me manage the disorder, including a drug that takes away the edges and delivers no downstream consequences.

One of the most potent discoveries for me has been meditation and mindfulness. In particular, daily practise of meditation, together with daily mindful practise, over one and a half years has provided the following benefits to me:

- A calmer way of being, leading to a reduction in stress.
- Ability to be more discriminative day to day, leading to sharper decision making.
- A greater sense of service to me and others resulting in a sustained focus on well-being in myself and others.
- A reduced sense of suffering followed by an increased sense of purpose.
- A much greater focus on what is important to me and my family.
- An increased ability to be in control of thoughts and emotions that used to be detrimental to my well-being.
- A much sharper sense of suffering in others and my own capacity to exhibit loving kindness.

I have now come across research to validate my own personal findings. There is a growing body of research occurring in this area acknowledging these and other benefits to mindfulness / meditation.

In summary, I am most grateful to have experienced such benefits and feel genuinely happier as a result.

This is clearly another doorway to have opened in my life, again offering new more powerful ways for me to observe myself and others.

From a mindfulness perspective, the start to my day includes:

1. An early morning walk where I contemplate three thoughts:
   a. What am I grateful for?
   b. Accepting the impermanence of life.
   c. What is meaningful to me and how will I respond today?
2. Recording my thoughts in journal or diary form.
3. Mindfulness meditation focusing on the breath (Shamatha) of around twenty-five to thirty minutes.
4. Exercise either in the gym or more walking throughout the day.

To know that I no longer need to be trapped by my thoughts and feelings is a liberating experience.

Activity Eight. Meditation

I invite you to consider the thirty days mindful life program, MLP, introduction to meditation program as a great starting point.

Details can be found on:
https://www.mindfullifenetwork.org/

Of course, there are many online sources for meditation; I find the Insight Timer App a most comprehensive library for guided meditations, training and support materials.

Gift Three: Actively balancing support of charity whilst cultivating wealth.

When Mark Molony and I established the consultancy company, diyLIFE Pty. Ltd, one of our tenets was that we would donate ten per cent of our earnings to community projects. This we did, supporting a number of community projects that otherwise would not have received help. This translated, for example, into a fifteen year relationship with the Rotary Youth Leadership Award (RYLA). That resulted in us facilitating leadership development workshops at each of their annual conferences for that period. Our work together also had the positive benefit of supporting many hundreds of young leaders in making a difference in the world.

This community focus stood on the shoulders of my earlier support for the Phoenix Park Community Playground project (Story P 6) and numerous posts on school committees. Additionally, there was my contribution as a scout leader, supporting boys and girls developing life and broader skills of learning.

In recent times my passion for making a direct, on the ground, contribution to community and charity has continued through the Chatterbox Bus, an outreach support charity for homeless youth on the streets of Melbourne. Additionally, my voluntary work as a board member and practitioner with Opening Doors, a charity and leadership development program to combat social isolation, was illuminating.

In Scotland, I have been able to stand on the shoulders of the transformational work I did as manager of the Monash Men's Shed, a highly successful sustainable Men's Shed in Australia. Five years ago, Charlie Traylor and I founded a brand-new charity. The Men of Leith Men's Shed in Edinburgh, Scotland. My role as co-founder and Chair allows me to help men to shift from isolation to connection, reclaiming purpose in their lives. With the reality of more people dying younger than they need to and dying of loneliness, our charity makes a significant difference and continues to grow.

What has been evident to me in donating a significant part of my time to community and charity is the immense sense of satisfaction I have derived from doing so. I experience a much greater sense of genuine happiness working as a volunteer on my charity than I did, for instance, in many roles where I was paid to work, yet experienced little or no satisfaction.

Genuine Happiness

The Mindful Life Program has introduced me to some fundamental discoveries around happiness, with one key distinction being the difference between stimulus driven pleasure and genuine happiness.

Alan B. Wallace, in an interview by the online publication, Tricycle, reminds us that we all know people in good health, love, wealth and fame who are miserable. I do recognise that pure happiness is more driven from being in service to others compared to short term gratification.

In terms of my personal interpretation, I believe generally that we can be happy and mostly this is driven by internal orientation, a focus, articulation, embodiment of values, aspirations and intentional activity. Yes, varied activity and creative activity in pursuit of goals and outcomes can enable genuine happiness.

I do believe that if we are engaged in a life of service, a more meaningful life, then we are more likely to experience the dimensions of happiness introduced above.

Matthieu Ricard jokes in his Ted Talk, www.matthieuricard.org, that we like suffering because it is so good when it ceases for a while. He goes further to say that we have a deep and profound desire for happiness and that to find it we need to look inward.

This experience, the experience of genuine happiness, revealed itself initially in a reaction to my final speech in Australia just short of my return to Scotland. In my leaving address to the folks at Monash Men's Shed, I delivered a crafted, heartfelt farewell. The audience stood, yes stood, as one and applauded with gusto. Later in the day, my son, Callum, called to say, "You have left your legacy in Australia, Dad." I felt an overwhelming sense of genuine happiness triggered by that remark and my own internal reflections.

This inward quest for genuine happiness seems to resonate. Please refer to the following activities in your book to determine where happiness may reside for you and how it might find a way into your gifts.

Activity Nine. Money & Happiness

How much money would you need to be genuinely happy?

What happiness would this money buy you?

What is the relationship between money and happiness for you?

What are the things that generate stimulus driven pleasure for you?

Activity Ten. Genuine Happiness

What does genuine happiness mean for you?

How will you know when you have genuine happiness?

Identify some stories from your life where you believe you were genuinely happy.

How can you create this again in your life?

How does stimulus driven pleasure differ from genuine happiness for you?

_____

_____

_____

_____

_____

_____

_____

_____

_____

Trust in God and Tie Up Your Ostriches.

The reason I tell you this story is to encourage you throughout your life to pause before making financial decisions and not allow yourself to be seduced by your, at times, delusional mind. By focussing on your financial well-being on a daily basis out of a spirit of making a broader difference in your community or the wider world, you have every opportunity to make a profit as well as make that difference.

Learning from our failures can most certainly be as palpable as learning from our achievements.

I share this story with you to illustrate a significant failure that in retrospect has provided great insight, ultimately resulting in greater financial freedom.

I was fortunate enough to spend a few days with the self-help guru I mentioned earlier, Anthony Robbins, www.tonyrobbins.com when he visited Sydney.

I can picture his big gleaming smile as he said, "Be your best always!" feeling that even though I was present with at least a thousand other folks, he was addressing me personally as he coached us in walking across burning hot coals. I can attest, they were red hot. I survived that challenge without incident but don't tell you this story to brag about this achievement at all.

> The reason I tell you this story is Robbins and others back then were tapping into a curiosity of potential with the thousands that attended his seminars, a curiosity around our capacity to do more, to be more.
>
> Unfortunately, at the time, this pursuit of potential was often misinterpreted or given too much precedence as an exclusive pursuit of financial or material gain.

Here, I am encouraging you to achieve your goals, financial or otherwise, within the context of experiencing genuine happiness. Within the context of experiencing your own gifts flourish.

I thought I was exploring my own improved financial potential when I made a disastrous decision in 1997. So compelling a story this is, that a friend of mine, Simon Hauser, would regularly tell this tale to new clients when he was operating as a financial advisor.

I mistook making a bold and creative financial decision with a view to taking proactive action on my fiscal future. In short, I bought an ostrich, swayed by the seductive arguments of the investment potential of these creatures. I invested over a thousand dollars in this venture, money I really could not afford to squander at the time, as we as a family had just re-located to work in Queensland, another State entirely, and our third child was due any moment.

Within just a few months of purchasing the said investment, I received notification that the bird had died. In reflection, there may not have been a bird in the first place! I had put energy and hard-earned cash into an investment that literally disappeared overnight.

The reason I tell you this story is the same reason that Simon tells the story to his clients. To remind them that, if you are to flourish financially or otherwise, your actions need to be underpinned by: thought, strategy, research and regular, deep consideration. Ideally there would also be an alignment with your values.

The consequences of this action for me at the time were really disastrous. You know that you are not travelling so well financially when you have to take back grocery items you have just placed on the checkout belt simply because you cannot afford them all.

This was a confronting learning that had a lifetime impact.

Thirty years later, having with my wife explored in detail how to generate wealth and carefully researched and deployed a myriad of strategies to achieve this, the learning has paid off.

We are now able to balance off wealth development with a substantial contribution to charity, all in pursuit of genuine happiness.

My reckless pursuit of short-term financial gain (stimulus driven pleasure) is a shadow of the past, a much richer context exists now. Now, carefully nurtured financial gain sits in the same equation as charitable and community contribution.

An important question for me now is, how can we be sustainably wealthy and continue to achieve genuine happiness?

Activity Eleven. Time to Pause and Re-calibrate, Then Act. Reflect on the activities you have completed so far, your core values, key life concerns and motivations, and focus on language. How you plan to be well, your thoughts on mindfulness and meditation and, of course, how you can achieve genuine happiness.

With this solid foundation, it is time now to create a draft of one of your gifts. You may already be clear as to what they will be or are going through a process of refining them.

Your task now is to write them down here, each one as an offer, as a declaration.

Again, consider your language in making this declaration. You would have already noted that my five gifts start with the words, 'I will'. A declaration as potent as a declaration of marriage. I will… Still it is your choice.

_____

_____

_____

_____

_____

_____

_____

_____

_____

Gift Four: Learning

Learning is of core importance to me.

Learning is critical to my existence and, I would suggest, vital to you. Whatever the domain, whatever the activity, skill or topic being explored. To be engaged in learning is to be alive. And to be open for learning, no matter how challenging, can also be liberating.

Firstly, I will include some breakthrough ideas that challenged conventional notions of how we learn. Then we will look to the world of ontology, the study of what it is to be human, to explore just how powerful moods and emotions can be in determining our capacity to engage as learners.

Multiple Intelligences

I wanted to include this theory, related as much to learning as it is to creativity. It is empowering because it challenges the once limited notion of intelligence and the reductive IQ scoring system. Howard Gardner's revolutionary theory of multiple intelligences allows us to explore where our preferences are whilst acknowledging that, like human gifts, our intelligence can be diverse.

I will include Gardner's early model where he identified seven intelligences, with a view to providing you with yet another opportunity to learn. Again, this knowledge can be applied in refining and strengthening your own gifts. If, of course, you want to learn more, I invite you to go to the source, Howard Gardner himself, https://howardgardner.com.

Activity Twelve. Multiple Intelligences
Map out your preferences in terms of your strength on each of the following intelligences.

For each of the seven intelligences below, read the descriptors and decide which three or four you are strongest in.

Then link these three or four to your emerging gifts. How do they add to your gifts or, indeed, how do your gifts add to them?

Linguistic – Generally, people who can read, write and talk effectively, e.g. like writing stories.

Logical / Mathematical – People who can manipulate figures, good at reasoning and logical analysis, e.g. like problem solving.

Musical – Good at sound, rhythms and composition, e.g. enjoys composing and performing.

Interpersonal – Strong in relating and understanding others, e.g. like conversing with others and groups.

Visual / Spatial – People with a strength here are good at visualising things and recognising patterns, e.g. can quite easily understand maps.

***Bodily Kinaesthetic** – Generally good at body movement and physical control, e.g. love sport.*

***Intrapersonal** – Self-awareness and introspection is high, e.g. clear as to own strengths and weaknesses.*

***Naturalistic** – More in tune with nature and the natural world, e.g. likely to explore a career as a biologist, zoologist or similar.*

Another benefit from exploring models like Howard Gardner's is that they remove the didactic notion of intelligence that existed previously. Rather than place a label that says we possess either low, high or medium Intelligent Quotient scores, here is a way that acknowledges and celebrates our differing learning gifts.

_____

_____

_____

_____

_____

_____

_____

_____

_____

Emotional Intelligence –
The Role of Moods and Emotions

So, what moods did you try on this morning? You have a choice with the clothes that you wear. Were you aware that you also have a choice with your moods? Let us try on a few to see what difference they make on how prepared we are for the day, what behaviours we choose to, or not to, engage in dependent on what moods we inhabit, whether chosen or habituated.

Activity Thirteen. The Six Pack of Human Moods
One of the models that I loved presenting to future leaders, teachers and community leaders was simply called the six pack of moods, informed by the breakthrough work of Fernando Flores, www.conversationsforaction.com. Alan Seiler also refers to Flores' model in his ontological coaching training programs and his three companion books on Coaching to the Human Soul, www.newfieldinstitute.com.au.

I am going to invite you now to try on each combination of the six moods as defined by Flores, an experiment in determining which of the six allow or restrict your suite of emotions and behaviours and capacity for learning. Of course, we could explore their application in many other contexts, yet for now, here are a few questions to assist you to get into each mood.

Take your pick from the six. Simply follow the written instructions to achieve an internal sense of that mood. The idea is to 'stand in' that mood, try it on as you would a new outfit or costume. I invite you to allow the mood to seep into you, embody it. As with any learning opportunity, the more you are willing to engage, the more you are likely to learn. Give it a shot.

1. Stand in a mood of Resentment.
You are fighting against something you just don't want to be true, though you know it is. You are trying to change the past, rage against it. How does this make you feel? How do you stand in this mood, how do you hold yourself?

How do you breathe?

What thoughts do you have? If you are invited to be part of a future project / conversation are you keen or not?

People talk about being bitter or angry in this mood. When you think of these emotions, how do they make you feel? What impact would they have on your behaviour?

2. Stand in a mood of Peace.
How do you stand?

When at peace, we have often accepted what has happened in the past.

How are you breathing in a state of peace?

What thoughts are most prominent?

If people were to engage you in a future project / conversation what might you say / do?

What impact does being at peace have on you?

3. Stand in a mood of Resignation.
How do you stand?

Beyond resentment, resignation is when we have given up; we may be present yet largely have shut down our contribution and effectively left the building.

How do you move when in resignation?

What thoughts exist mostly? What emotions exist for you?

If people were to engage you in a future project / conversation what might you say / do?

What impact does resignation have on you, on your behaviour?

Resignation is fuelled by the notion that there is no point, there is simply no possibility. As much of my book so far has included personal stories of possibility and potential, it is important to consider that we could easily all have been impacted by this limiting and, at times, unseen mood.

4. Stand in a mood of Ambition.

How do you stand, what is your physiological expression of ambition? Your feet, your hands, your head, how you hold your expression, your facial features?

What thoughts are most present in ambition?

What impact does ambition have on you, on your behaviour?

What emotions do you engage with? What emotions are suppressed?

How do you feel in this mood?

5. Stand in a mood of Anxiety.

What would we see if we were to observe you embodying anxiety?

What are you thinking? Not thinking?

If people were to engage you in a future project / conversation what might you say / do?

Breathe as if you are anxious. What do you notice?

Our final mood, wonder, is often seen as an antidote to anxiety.

6. Stand in the mood of Wonder.
What would we see if we were to observe you embodying wonder? What age do you depict yourself as most wonderous?
What are you thinking as you embrace wonder?
If people were to engage you in a future project / conversation what might you say / do?
How is your breathing when in wonder?

I invite you to contemplate the above exercises in embodying a few of the six core moods. Can you observe times in your life when you may have been caught in some of these moods without even realising?

Of course, certain mood states exist for a reason and are appropriate at certain times of our life, for example response to death or in times of crisis. However, there is no requirement to have such moods hang around longer than they need to.

The main point here, of course, is whilst it is possible to be thrown to particular moods, often those not so useful for us, it is important to realise that we do have a choice.

If you consider that the choice of moods we embrace in our lives dictates so much of our behaviours, then it is pertinent that we regularly decide which moods we are going to wear today. Or, what is the appropriate emotional response in a given situation?

This alone will significantly impact the quality of your engagement with yourself and others and assist you in articulating and living your gifts.

Gift Five: Creativity

I embrace Creativity, actively engaging in creative pursuits that stretch my creative expression.

Not simply a way to wake up our brains, creativity can provide meaning and purpose in our lives. Whether randomly splashing some paint on a canvas, crafting the next Harry Potter series or singing with abandon, creative pursuits are all around you and await your participation.

We will all be aware of stories on creativity and its impact on the brain and well-being. Whether it be singing as a strategy to help dementia patients recall key times in their lives, or the power of art in communicating complex ideas. Creativity works.

The following story is one of my myriad blogs and I include it in this book purely as a piece of entertainment for you. I have used creative expression for many purposes to date including personal therapy and can vouch for the many benefits writing and, indeed, singing has had on my life.

Please enjoy, 'Men and Women of Rock Choir – We Salute You!'

For those unfamiliar with Edinburgh, there is a statue to Wee Bobbie, a truly loyal Skye terrier outside Greyfriars Kirk. Wee Bobbie was so inseparable from his master, Auld Jock, he guarded his graveside years after Jock's death in 1858 and now has his own gravestone outside the church.

Wee Bobby's nose twitches ever so slightly, his squidgy eyes gradually open to take in the churchyard. His delightfully scruffy face is focused, a picture of curiosity, amplified by a slight tilt, a little to the left. The secret is revealed as he detects sounds from the Kirk, his Kirk. After all he is Greyfriars Bobby. He listens with the cute attentiveness you see only in terriers.

'Ladies and Gentlemen, I am delighted to introduce you to the Men of Edinburgh Rock Choir'. Elaine's introduction is compelling and the applause warms chilled bones. Ten willing men proudly walk up the spine of the church and take their place in front of the ninety-fold Edinburgh Rock Choir members. For the first time in Edinburgh, their hometown, among their ain folk, they poise to perform.

Mark's delightful treatment on the piano nurtures 'Hold Back the River', a soulful song by James Bay. The boys deliver accordingly. It went down a treat at the Glasgow Concert Hall last Saturday with three sold out shows and here they are singing from their souls in this iconic church, packed for the event. As one of the choristers commented, "It was a lovely rich sound." Aye it was that.

Wee Bobby agreed, listening carefully and getting ready to put on some moves in the next set. You see Rock Choir is more than just singing. There are moves and routines that are generally quite challenging to the male members and, of course, Wee Bobby himself.

Still, like us he wants to step up to the mark. The Men of Edinburgh Rock Choir threaded their way back into the whole choir to strong applause, there were two songs remaining for this evening's performance before the finale. 'Can't Stop the Feeling' and 'Don't Stop Me Now', were exuberantly performed, with intensity and zing.

Before the male performance, Dylan, wheelchair bound, used his electronic device to communicate with the audience, not unlike Steven Hawking. He explained just how much a positive impact this choir had to his life and how supportive everyone was of him, seeing beyond his disability. I was singing next to Dylan in the final performance, a real privilege.

The inclusion of this young man and the simple acceptance of all people to participate in the choir, sing, laugh and enjoy is particularly gratifying. Here is an organisation genuinely committed to embodying core human values.

It is not unusual to see CEO and founder, Caroline Redman, appearing on UK television with choir members. She speaks enthusiastically about choir events, a recent one being the opening performance at the BBC Proms in the Park in Hyde Park in London. Choir leaders onstage led close to ten thousand Rock Choir members offstage, performing a flash mob to 'Dancing in the Streets'.

Back to Greyfriars and Elaine proudly indicates that there were twenty-eight thousand members of Rock Choirs UK wide. Quite amazing, an offer that resonates and is enjoyed by so many.

'It was excellent, thoroughly enjoyable!' a dear friend commented. There were smiles, there was joy and some folks were moved to tears. It disnae get any better than that!

The final song of the evening, 'Hallelujah', was hauntingly beautiful. Incorporating the merged talents of sopranos, altos, and basses, this intoxicating song left a respectful imprint on the Kirk. I do believe it would have 'pleased the Lord'.

Wee Bobby was awfy pleased, happy to be woken from his earlier dwams. He tilted his cute, scruffy head to the right, shed a wee tear and went straight back to sleep.

Men and women of Edinburgh Rock Choir, your leaders and supporters, we salute you!

My preference to sing, write and draw colourful images and mind maps certainly add dimensions to my life I could never have imagined.

Since that performance, our Rock Choir has travelled to Paris to sing at the Eiffel Tower, performed often at the Edinburgh International Festival and even sang the National Anthem at the opening to the International Hockey competition here in Scotland. This is truly inspirational to me and I sense will again be a source of genuine happiness. Just like the smaller, but just as rewarding, concert we gave to Inch Old People's Home recently, where residents and carers smiled, sang and danced along to our choir. A truly joyful experience. The gift of song returned with the gift of love. Genuine happiness on parade.

Doors are opening yet again for me and this time my creative gifts are flooding through.

Activity Fourteen. Creativity
'The chief enemy of creativity is good sense'. Pablo Picasso

Use this double page space to take on the Picasso challenge. Use it to express in words, colours, music or any other way you can think of, the gifts you choose to offer in life. Be as creative as you choose in your depictions.

Activity Fifteen. Refine Your Gifts
In summary, it is time for you to reflect on the contents of this book so far, the inspirational stories and practical examples, as you now:
1. *Refine your own gifts, and*
2. *Do so in a way that will resonate with you and the people you offer them to.*

Use Activities 1 to 15 above as a guide. Consider each of them again and then start work capturing them in a way you can present them to others.

Refine and document your first few gifts.

Choose an image that fits with your proposed life gifts.
How does the image represent your gifts?
Why do you think the image resonates with you?
Show it to a friend, what do they think?
Create statements that as clearly as possible articulate your life gifts. If it helps, start with 'I will...' or simply 'I intend...'.

Refer to the many additional examples below for more ideas and tips to help you.

_____

_____

_____

_____

_____

Additional Special Gifts to Help You Make it all Happen.

Each of these carefully selected strategies and examples will provide assistance as you finalise your gifts, refine them and live them. Each of them helps you to consolidate, clarify and record.

- Circles of Influence & Concern – Making choices based on reality
- Conditions of Satisfaction – Understanding what others expect
- Conversation / Connection / Collaboration – Enrolling others
- Learning from our youth leaders. Compelling stories

Circles of Influence and Concern

In order to optimise your exploration into your gifts and areas of life you choose to focus on, I invite you to consider the gifts of Stephen Covey again and his model, circles of influence and concern.

Covey encouraged us to consider where it makes best sense for us to focus our attention, choosing our actions carefully in pursuit of our gifts.

I have created an activity for you based on his model in the spirit of you maximising the use of your time and energy moving forward. To quote Covey, he encourages us to avoid 'getting caught in the thick of thin things'.

Activity Sixteen. Circles of Influence
Create a list of all the areas requiring attention in relation to one or more of your gifts.

You will note that two large circles have been drawn and are labelled.

Now take all of the areas requiring attention you have listed for this exercise and others that occur in the moment. Put them into either the inside or outside circles or beyond.

What you are left with is the beginnings of a plan. So many people spend too much time attempting to change things that are simply not in their control. Remember the activity on moods we considered earlier. If we were to allow ourselves to be caught in the mood of resentment, we may feel trapped in the circle we have no control over. We might spend so much of our life putting energy or angst into this space.

Where does it make sense for you to invest your energy in bringing your gifts to life?

Start with what you can influence and what is in your control, and you may find that your circles expand. Again, linking back to the exercise on moods, what moods are useful for you to nurture in gaining influence and control?

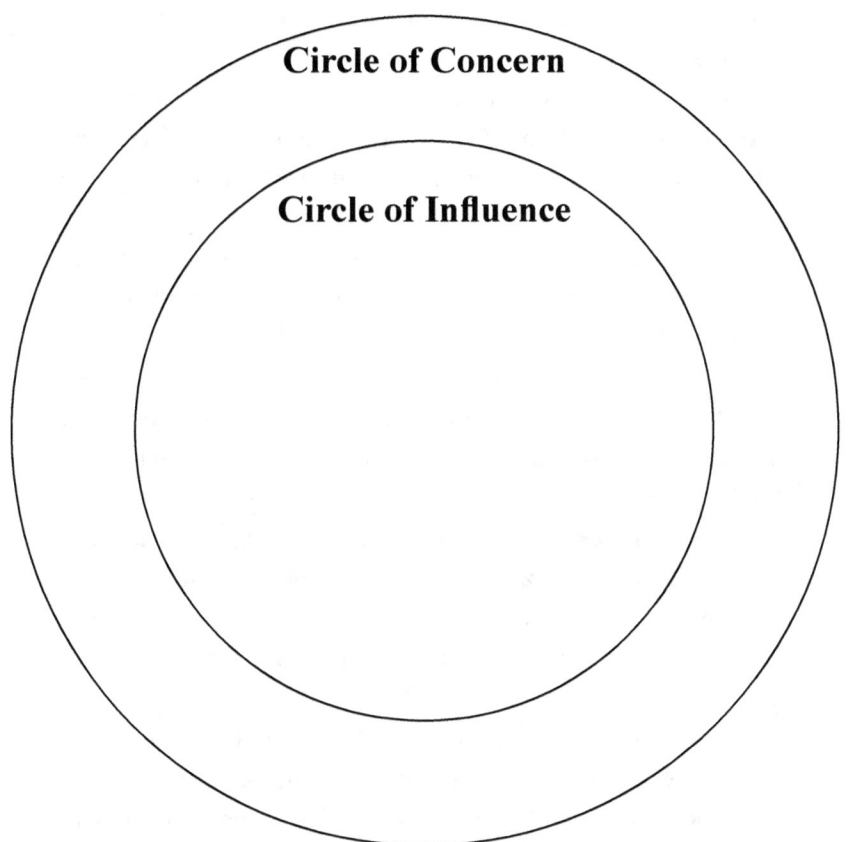

Conditions of Satisfaction

What is the meaning of your message? If it is your intent with your own life to deliver on the needs of others, how do we know what others need? We all have certain criteria or conditions of satisfaction that we apply to all aspects of our life. We possess our own internal ratings system that we apply to just about everything.

Imagine you are in a café you have never visited before and are just about to order your favourite beverage. It may be a flat white, pot of tea or piccolo, regardless, the staff member has just taken your order.

Now, from this point on, what is your expectation from purely a timing perspective that your beverage will be delivered?

Whatever you indicate, whether it be five minutes, seven minutes, ten minutes or perhaps more, this is your condition of satisfaction around drink delivery time. Everyone has some kind of expectation and they differ enormously.

The point here is such a simple construct as drink delivery time we can have such varying conditions of satisfaction. Imagine if we add temperature, taste, quality of crockery, the barista's behaviour or indeed the cleanliness of the tables. Of course, the list is endless.

Again, I include this seemingly meaningless example to emphasise the significant task we have in delivering on our own and others' conditions of satisfaction. Ideally, we would like others to choose our offers, our gifts because they align to their conditions of satisfaction.

Activity Seventeen. Conditions of Satisfaction

Think of the criteria that you apply to more important issues in your life than simply the acquisition of a coffee. What about relationships. What are your conditions of satisfaction when it comes to being a good:

Father?
Mother?
Spouse?
Friend?

How do you think your criteria match up with family members? Identify your own conditions then ask two or three members of your family, or close friends.

The only way we can know what others' conditions of satisfaction are is by understanding them, by eliciting them and by listening carefully to the answers. We can be clear on our own conditions, but if we are to create gifts that resonate with others and in collaboration with them, we must embrace others' interpretations.

Holidays are important to us, often gifts in themselves. Many of us have a limited amount of time each year where we can have a break from our day to day activities and have some travel experiences. Not surprisingly many of us have high expectations when it comes to a trip away. Living in Edinburgh we were very much looking forward to three weeks in Italy. We had travelled with the same company, the year before and were impressed enough to book again. This time though we would be more than impressed, we would be delighted. All down to one man, our amazing guide Flavio Lazaretto. This young man was enthusiastic, energetic and determined to understand and deliver on the needs of all twelve folks on our trip. In short, not only did he meet our conditions of satisfaction, he exceeded them.

    The final day of our trip was a prime example. At a sumptuous lunch in a delightful winery Flavio presented a gift to each traveller, an individual photo captured during the trip on the back of which he provided a unique thank you note, outlining the value each of us brought to the trip. To top that off, as we arrived in Florence to end the trip, Flavio offered to introduce us to a local restaurant, one of his favourites. He was already off duty and had a train to catch to Padua, yet still continued to provide exceptional service.

    Not surprisingly many of us on that trip stayed in contact with Flavio and returned to Italy to be the first on his own tour of his homeland, Venetian Explorer tour, goldeneyediscoveries.com. Of course, now running his own business, Flavio again exceeded our conditions of satisfaction. We look forward to more European tours with Flavio as our guide.

Activity Eighteen. Conditions of Satisfaction
Consider your own ratings system for some important aspects of your life. Are there aspects that fit within your life gift? Ask for input from others where you can. This can be an illuminating exercise.

Choose some different domains of life to explore. For example, what are your conditions of satisfaction when it comes to:

Health, Health Care
Professionalism
Wealth
Entertainment

Your ideas from here can be transferred to your earlier activities when you are ready.

_____

_____

_____

_____

_____

_____

_____

_____

Three elements in living your gifts:
Conversation, Collaboration & Community

As a facilitator of change and transformation I am often called on to bring people together to determine a common purpose and leave them empowered to bring that purpose to life, often through a matrix of detailed strategies and action plans. I stress the importance of conversation, connection, collaboration and community as powerful ways to make your gifts sing.

Conversation

I mentioned earlier, as informed by the linguists, that conversation is critical in our development as human beings. We only relate through language which includes internal language, body language as well as words. The more adept we are at using our language in encouraging our fellow human beings to work together in achieving projects of significance, the more able we are to actually achieve these projects.

One of the earliest community projects I worked on when my kids were attending a local primary school, helped me see the importance of conversation, relationships and communication. Together these three components combine to create transformation.

Twenty years later, I returned to Malvern Valley Primary School in the south eastern suburbs of Melbourne, Australia. The comprehensive community-built playground that we planned for over a year and built in only a week, stands proud, still servicing the community and completely free of damage or graffiti.

There are turrets, slides, tunnels and swings, all inspired by the children's designs and built with a workforce of around one thousand five hundred beautiful people all on a shoestring budget. Why no graffiti, no damage? It was built by and therefore is owned by the community. The community simply look after it.

Clever conversations allowed us, the Project Leadership Team to accept control of the project from the Local Council. They had previously wanted to support a proposal to give the site to developers to develop more medium density housing. This site was previously Chadstone Secondary School and was sold off by the State Government to raise funds for infrastructure projects.

Careful conversation preserved that site as a community park, it now has not only the playground but also a kindergarten, library, skate park and community centre.

Choreographed conversation engaged many people, contractors and residents to donate their tools, their skills and their time to work with focus on the project.

At times, challenging conversations were required to ensure that the project was delivered on time, on budget and according to quality parameters.

It was, and always is, clever, careful, choreographed and at times challenging conversations that are required if we are to achieve extraordinary things. Things that twenty years on are still flourishing.

In the spirit of nurturing quality conversations, I offer the following distinctions.

Language in action

Have you ever heard of the term: 'You can't take the milk out of the tea'? In other words, once you have uttered something, it cannot be unuttered or unheard. As you refine your own gifts, the simple process of declaring these puts them like the milk, into the tea of life. A declaration is action in itself, it is an intention.

So, think carefully about what you choose to declare, what you choose to enact.

Activity Nineteen.
Create three declarations linked to your already identified gifts. Articulate how you intend to enact them. What specifically (remember SMART) will you do to make them happen?

Types of Conversations

One of the delightful opportunities that I derived from studying ontology, the study of what it is to be human, was studying conversations. I was surprised to discover that, in the field of conversations and conversational actions, scholars had identified not just one form of conversation but many. Immediately, I found through this study that my vocabulary increased. As did my capacity to learn broader forms of conversation, whilst sharpening my existing ones.

As a consultant in business, it was often useful to clarify that our planning meeting would be a combination of speculative conversations and conversations for action. It was necessary to remind organisational leaders that sometimes a balance was necessary for new ideas / processes / products to emerge from the planning meeting before taking the action necessary to turn these ideas into action.

One such conversation based on the Open Space process helped save a charitable organisation, Opening Doors, from having to close its doors. Key stakeholders were invited to a conversation for speculation which was invested in generating ideas and opportunities for keeping the charity active. Later in the session, plans were agreed to go forward. This resulted in attracting energy and support to the charity at a critical time. Ultimately, this led to the charity finding the necessary funds for its sustainable continuation.

Over six years on from that critical conversation, Opening Doors is thriving; it has created over two hundred community leaders and continues to play a vital role in 'connecting an estimated twenty thousand people in their communities in new and positive ways'. It is truly amazing what can be created from intentional conversations.

Activity Twenty. Types of conversations
What are you embracing – what could you be embracing?

Conversations for speculation – Great for generating ideas; there is no pressure to find solutions in speculative conversations.

Conversations for relationship – Many relationships would be saved if people took time out to explore the health of their relationship.

Conversations for clarity – Critical in business, a shared understanding of what is to be achieved and how is very important.

Conversations for action – Gaining clarity around what specifically is to be achieved.

Conversation & Community

Of course, the earlier examples of building Phoenix Park Community Playground and assisting Opening Doors continue as a charity are highly practical examples of conversation in action with transformational outcomes.

The process of engaging people in both these projects is not unlike the Open Space Technology process pioneered by Harrison Owen. Open Space Technology is a means of organizing and running meetings or conferences with small to large numbers of participants, encouraging and validating participation and decision making.

The revered author, Marvin Weisbord, indicates that if we want change to happen, we should aim to get as many folks in the organisation in the one room and at the same time. Similar principles sit behind Open Space Technology, where the notion is that whoever turns up to the event are just the right people. The space is set for powerful conversations to be had because participation is validated from the get go.

Alan (who likes to be called Al) Stewart, PhD, is an experienced facilitator of Open Space and other conversational processes used to address complex matters. In the past decade, however, he has turned his attention to hosting a new conversational process in the form of social gathering in which participants engage with, and about, each other.

This happens in what he has called Conversare – from the Latin con versare –to turn or to dance together. Events are held in public places. Anyone who wishes to come along is welcome. This brings strangers together in a way in which they engage in wonderful conversations. Which highlights the amazing possibilities that are triggered when strangers have this kind of spirited, respectful engaging.

As Al says, **Conversare** events are,

'Hosted events in which participation – by everyone present – is to experience listening and speaking with full attention to how each other see life. In other words, to explore their common humanity'. In a way, described by a participant as, "Simple and deep, a spiritual adventure."

This is different from 'meet-up' events in that here the focus is not about addressing an issue or a topic. Instead, the essence is mainly to get to know something about your dinner partner such as 'Who are you'? 'What attracts you to be here'? 'What are your main interests'? 'What brings you most alive'?

This is specifically not about 'What do you do'?

The events happen over a shared meal, an ancient practice of hospitality.

A host provides some simple guidelines to facilitate the conversation among which are 'Whoever comes are the right people' and 'Do you appreciate that we are here to give, rather than get?'.

This new way of socialising was invented when Alan was living happily in Hong Kong for six years until 2011. Where it was reported by many participants, English speaking local people and expats, to be remarkably interesting and enjoyable. Since being back in Australia, these events have been held mainly in the Adelaide Central Market after trading hours on weekday evenings.

Participants are often buoyant in their feedback.

'A wonderful and refreshing experience of encounter with others who care deeply about community. It has inspired me to host a similar regular conversation in my own community and share the concept with other community builders across the globe… Thanks, Alan, for your passion and commitment'.

Peter Kenyon | Director, Bank of Initiatives for the Development of Enterprising Action & Strategies (I.D.E.A.S.)

The Shape of Things to Come - Gifts in Action, Already Flourishing.

It was often our final activity that resonated deeply with the young leaders, that inspired them to take action. Throughout the day Mark Molony and I took them through a number of activities that had them question their offer as a leader to themselves and their communities. We walked them through the values exercise included in this text, helping to determine clarity and motivation for the future.

Embodiment of the moods exercise also included in this text often challenged them with the discovery that they fundamentally had choice around their own moods regardless of what was occurring around them.

Our exploration of 'What makes your heart sing' was also powerful and fruitful, requiring a deep reflection and articulation of core aspirations, rarely considered.

Back to the final activity and not an easy one to facilitate. Each young leader would take a place in a line typically across a football field. Using a combination of suggestopedic language and guided meditation they were invited to envisage themselves in a future typically one or two years hence. This they would do in detail immersing all senses. When totally immersed we invited them to clap and walk to their imagined future at the other end of the sports ground. For many this was the most memorable activity in RYLA as it delivered such clarity and motivation for their future.

Blending these and other transformational tools established a solid basis for the young leaders to stand on the shoulder of their learnings from other presenters and ready themselves to make change happen in their own lives and the lives of others.

In short, they were able to clarify their own gifts and had a framework to put these into action. Sound familiar?

The three stories I include here represent genuine leadership enacted by our young people demonstrating their many and varied gifts.

I have provided ample examples and carefully created stories to emphasise how important discovering and living your gifts can be and of course, many tools for you to get started. So, like our RYLA friends, my invitation to you now is to use their inspiration and simply get started.

Briallen Davies, a 2014 Graduate of RYLA, shared with Linda Gidlund, one of the directors of the program and now leader for RYLA Oceana, her enthusiasm about the program and how it has provided clarity and direction for her.

"Me? Well, to start with, I am playing music again. I haven't played since Feb 2009. I am studying for the "Graduate Entry Medical School Aptitude Test" and, one day I will be a doctor. I volunteer regularly, and am so much more positive. I am taking care of my health and wellbeing, as well as being more environmentally friendly. I am making our community a better place, and I am helping people, in my own way; which is something that I plan on continuing with!

So, at the risk of sounding disgustingly corny, RYLA has been a game changer for me. Not only this, but I know it has been a game changer for so many other people. I now have the most supportive, encouraging, hilariously diverse group of new friends and I finally have a sense of direction!

I am so much happier, and definitely much more grateful for everything that I have. I whole heartedly endorse this program for anybody fortunate enough to be offered the opportunity to participate in the future."

We can all learn from Briallen's comments regarding self-awareness. Much of the earlier chapters of this book are designed to allow us to become more self-aware, more able to be attuned to our strengths and our potential areas of development. Our quest to be our best is a continual pursuit, we are continually sharpening our skills, as Briallen infers.

Recently, Linda Gidlund interviewed Ludovic Grosjean, an impressive graduate of RYLA. She discovered that Ludovic, a mechatronics engineer and oceanographer who supports business and government in the design of environmental and monitoring solutions, has a passion for cleaning up ocean pollution by tracing it to the source.

Before attending RYLA, he saw no prospect of getting ahead or out of his current situation, feeling he was floundering in life.

He learnt from the RYLA program that achieving goals is not the act of completing one thing, it is a continuous series of activities and tasks, achieved over time with a bit of effort every day.

Using this strategy, Ludovic founded a Clean Up the Yarra project, with a unique approach, using volunteers to implement the project and using a technical approach to clean up ocean pollution. The Yarra is Melbourne, Australia's most significant river and I can attest to how polluted it became, being a regular cyclist along its banks.

Ludovic made many presentations to Rotary clubs in

pursuit of his vision, achieving significant support from the Rotary District Governor and ultimately being awarded, setting him on a journey of change.

His acknowledgements for this journey are numerous.

He was awarded the Bolloré Award in 2011 and the IEEE Award in 2013 for his work in ocean engineering.

In 2018, Ludovic was selected by Barry Rassin, President of Rotary International, to be named 'Rotary's People of Action: Young Innovator'.

Ludovic is one of six young innovators to showcase his work at the United Nations in Nairobi, Kenya on November 10th, 2018 and is a 2018 Finalist of the Young Entrepreneur Award in Melbourne

As a supporter of Rotary values, Ludovic has been providing an innovative approach to clean water. As a leader and community educator, he strives for projects to reduce water pollution on a global scale and to make a long-term difference for humanity. His career focus is to build collaboration between organizations in order to advance engineering and preserve the environment, with the ultimate goal of saving our oceans.

My youngest son, Elliot, also a graduate of RYLA and past President of Rotaract Edinburgh, has been highly involved since 2015 in developing the Edinburgh club. He describes the compelling impact that community engagement on a local and global level has had on his personal development and learning, and contribution to the world.

Back in Melbourne, Australia, Elliot joined forces with the recent Order of Australia recipient, Shashi Kumar, in a neat little initiative. Every week, my car smelled so sweetly of bread products as a result of the Bread Run project. Shashi, Elliot and my middle son, Duncan, also a graduate of RYLA, arranged with a team of good willed folks to pick up bread at the end of the trading day from a number of bakeries in Melbourne. They then delivered them first thing in the morning, still quite fresh, to a range of charities. My charity, the Monash Men's Shed, was one of the recipients; the men just loved that delivery of bread which for many was a staple product they could not otherwise have afforded.

The Bread Run serves as a simple example, yet again, of how clever conversations and an intent to collaborate can and does help serve community. Bread products that would have ended up in the bin ended up on the tables of those most in need of them.

Safe to say it is folks like Shashi, Elliot and Duncan whose simple spirit of care and intent make such a big difference. A hearty congratulation to the bakery chain, Bakers Delight, who were most helpful in facilitating the project.

I include these examples in this text as a reminder that, if our gifts are aligned in some way with others, requiring input or collaboration, we can achieve significant outcomes like the stories featured. It is essential we become great conversationalists, capable of enrolling people in our connected communities.

I am convinced that you will understand why Mark Molony and I supported RYLA on a voluntary basis for so many years. The graduates of the program continue to deliver great solutions for their communities whilst discovering and living their unique gifts.

This last activity may just provide one final trigger to bring your gifts to life. Think about the difference our young leaders are making and consider what you could create in your own community.

Activity Twenty-one.
Brainstorm, ideally with others, possibilities for community engagement in your area.
What is already happening?
What is missing?
What could you create?
Where are you?
What would you have to do to make it happen?
Create a map of your community, include everything, everyone that exists. What are the links that exist between people and groups? What could exist?

_____

_____

_____

_____

_____

_____

_____

_____

Presenting Your Gifts

You have carefully selected your gifts; you know they will be more than palatable. You have applied appropriate wrapping, being aware that it is merely a vehicle for the gift itself, not the actual gift.

Your gift is ready, it is pristine and awaits unveiling.

This is your time to enjoy the anticipation, that moment, that small, yet delicious moment before you take the leap. It will be more than a leap of faith, more than a leap into the unknown given your spirit of care and attention in crafting it.

But still there is that moment of anticipation. Enjoy it and be bold as the packaging is either carefully or rapidly removed revealing, yes, revealing you. The refined, the congruent, the future you.

Offer your gifts, your future to yourself.

Offer them to others.

Be prepared to learn and flourish.

Well Being!
Alan Forsyth
www.followingforsyth.com

A Final Request

I would be grateful if you would share your experiences in reading this book with me, your reactions to Five Gifts Flourishing and the gifts you have identified for yourself. This will contribute to my learning and in designing future offers that help people reduce suffering and lead a flourishing life.
alan@followingforsyth.com

References

It is very important to me to acknowledge the sources I refer to in Five Gifts Flourishing and I invite you to follow up for a more detailed appreciation of their contribution to my learning.

- Bandler, Richard; Grinder, John. The Structure of Magic I: A Book about Language and Therapy. (1975)
- Briggs-Myers, Isabel, and Peter B. Myers. Gifts differing: Understanding Personality Type. (1995)
- Burns, Dr Stephanie, Great Lies We Live By. (2010)
- Covey, Stephen R., and Sean Covey. The 7 habits of highly effective people. (2020)
- Gardener, H, Multiple Intelligences. (1983)
- Hargraves, R. Mr Busy. (1978)
- Harrison, Owen, Open Space Technology: A users Guide. (2008)
- Lozanov, Georgi, Suggestology and Outlines of Suggestopedy. (1978)
- Robbins, A. Awaken the Giant Within. (1986)
- Stern, D, G. Wittgenstein, on Mind and Language. (1995)
- Wallace Allan, B. The Attention Revolution. (2006)
- Weisbord, M, Productive Workplaces. (1992)

Websites

- Bakers Delight – www.bakersdelight.com.au
- Beyond Blue - www.beyondblue.org.au
- Flavio – www.goldeneyediscoveries.com
- Following Forsyth – The author's website – www.followingforsyth.com
- Men of Leith Men's Shed - www.leithmensshed.org
- Mindful Life Program - www.mindfullifeprogram.org
- Monash Men's Shed – www.monashshed.org.au
- Opening Doors Leadership Program - www.linkhc.org.au/opening-doors
- Permanent Domains of Human Concern – Fernando Flores & Michael Graves. www.gerry.wagn.org/Permanent_Domains_of_Human_Concern
- Rotary Youth Leadership Award – www.ryla9790.org
- Rock Choir – www.rockchoir.co.uk
- Alan Seiler – www.newfieldinstitute.com.au
- Scottish Men's Shed Association – www.smsa.co.uk
- Alan Stewart – www.conversare.net
- Victorian Men's Shed Association – www.vmsa.org.au

www.ingramcontent.com/pod-product-compliance
Lightning Source LLC
LaVergne TN
LVHW020414070526
838199LV00054B/3611